# Shams

*by only human*

Peggy Goldreich

INDIA • SINGAPORE • MALAYSIA

Copyright © Peggy Goldreich 2023
All Rights Reserved.

ISBN 979-8-89133-812-8

This book has been published with all efforts taken to make the material error-free after the consent of the author. However, the author and the publisher do not assume and hereby disclaim any liability to any party for any loss, damage, or disruption caused by errors or omissions, whether such errors or omissions result from negligence, accident, or any other cause.

While every effort has been made to avoid any mistake or omission, this publication is being sold on the condition and understanding that neither the author nor the publishers or printers would be liable in any manner to any person by reason of any mistake or omission in this publication or for any action taken or omitted to be taken or advice rendered or accepted on the basis of this work. For any defect in printing or binding the publishers will be liable only to replace the defective copy by another copy of this work then available.

*Dedicated to my soul family*
*The ones who help me through this life*

# Author's Preface

"Who says the immortal one has died?"

"Who says the "sun" of hope has died?"

Rumi-The Veil pg 104

Finally the Bird started to understand
who I was.
I called Rumi the bird
because I made him sing love
for the whole world.
He called me the Sun

I am Shams al-Din Mohammad
never born–never died
from Tabriz
I am a weaver of baskets
A wanderer and a writer

May I open the door?

Truly, I am an ascended master of soul travel.
This book is about how I teach,
to become, be and unite a world
that has always been in conflict
Conflict because everything is put before LOVE

I embrace you all in love
and say wherever you are in time
and space your soul carries the light of love
for you always
It is time to look inside and bring love out

Shams
ليكن

## Awake

I descend to Be with You

I ascend for the next soul encounter

## Shams intro

Oh! All people of the earth!
You have been enslaved for so long
Look for the light
It is simple and everywhere
Honor your light
a gift you brought from heaven
Look at the soil and grow ideas
for a new world
Feel your feet on the earth and
inhale the roots you have always had
Now is the time
I, Shams will help you see miracles
I will build you up inside
where no other can enter
You will then be a warrior of the light
Because power is inside you
The truth has been kept from you
Truth is for all and inside all

Why have you not taken time to look?
You are so distracted
Your head is filled with noise
but the music of your soul plays continuously
Be silent and hear your heart
the magnet that will bring you closer to truth
The truth returns again and again
trying  to keep the negative out of your heart
Watch your thoughts
Watch your words
Watch your emotions
they are powerful weapons
Before thinking, stand back and honor the enemy
Honor the others and honor yourself

*Silence is neutral and the energy of the*
*universe will keep the balance*

*Believe*
*You are a gift of the creator*
*soul of 3 million years*
*A body that travels from life to life*
*Call on your intelligence*
*The intelligence of the earth*
*the sky*
*the seas*
*All mixed inside you*
*You man of heaven and earth*

*Your Dreams*
*the parallel world where you can be You*
*You the creator of your world*
*Kneel down to your gift of You*
*for there was never any other meaning for life*
*but joy and happiness*
*And now it will begin*
*And so it is!*
*And so it is!*
*And so it is!*

*Shams*

# Shams 1

Oh my son!
I will make you sing like a bird
This song will reach into infinity
The symbols of my love touch your soul
Those who feel with the heart
treasures are found
when the seeker is wise
The true seeker will never give up
looking for the answers of his being
The bird is a symbol
of the instinctive song of your universe
Inside yourself you have this song
and many more
Go inside
dance until ecstasy brings out the best in you
You are the symbol of my love
for this moment in time

# Shams 2

They know me in other realms as the Mahanta
I come to you in the dimension of 5
Your initiation is the Ray of Light
that is created by the universe
Unknowing you will give messages
of great insight
Knowingly you will live in delight
And those around you
will be exalted by your precision of words
The Ray of the Godhead descends upon you
The qualities of the Divine
Divine Will
Divine Love
Divine Wisdom
enter your path
And your writing of verse
Will be of the divine
Made for those on earth for reflection

Gratitude is the key for our arrival
Joy is the energy for the journey
Do not tire
for there will be times when faith is low
but
There is always one that loves you dearly
and
Can give you the will to go on

## Shams 3

I dwell in simplicity
I dance with the universe
What are words?
Libraries outside ourselves have covered
our words
with words of others
We distract ourselves with the ways of others
Ever repeating the sorrows
and darkness lived many years ago
Improvise your dancing
Dance to the music with your expression of love
Go inside and whatever you feel will be of self
Each layer has a new explanation for you
Question it
For the three gifts I give you on your way are
-imagination
-attention
-the power of concentration
Make each of these a dance of their own
and you will become the master
I see in you

# Shams 4

You have been imprisoned
in the flesh of your worldly existence
My feelings are not like yours
Light is everywhere
Your darkness cannot touch me.
I could tell you many stories of soul travel
You never look inside to find me
why not?
With love you may see me twinkle
With laughter
I vibrate from you
What pleasure to see how the waves of emotion
flow from your heart
This is why I protect you
You are here to save others from themselves
A symbol of unconditional Love
Compassion for the depressed
Security for insecure
A teacher of life
I give you this
This is my soul responsibility now
Many will shun the sweetness
But after many years there will arise
an energy on earth that will thirst for your words
It will be a time of chaos but change will flow
Your words will be understood
not only in the head
but
they will move the heart like the dance you do
each day
picking the words out of your soul

## Shams 5

*On stage before your followers*
*we will make the unreal - real*
*For what is unreal dwells*
*in a different part of our emotions*
*far away from the thunder*
*of the world around us*
*Through human emotions*
*we ride a wave of high and low vibrations*
*This wave changes*
*with pull and the push like the tides of the ocean*
*When high*
*we meet the angels and the masters of love*
*When low,*
*we fall into darkness*
*with the kings of the underworld*
*Balancing emotions*
*is worth understanding*
*When you twirl on one foot*
*balance is necessary ...*
*but concentration on one foot is meaningless*
*You must give your emotion to the higher wave*
*and the dance becomes a direct connection to joy*
*Oh how sweet emotions are to us*
*presenting our heart with love, joy and*
*playfulness*
*The unreal mythos that connects us to the angels*
*and to the realm of all that is waiting for us*
*But ....how bitter they may become when we*
*sink deep in an ocean of despair*

*Shams 6*

# *Silence!*

*It is in silence I can fill the void*
*with your poems.*
*In silence there is only feeling*
*Shhhhhhhhhhhhh................................ . . . .   .*

## Shams 7

*With your imagination*
*I create with you*
*If you allow me*
*I will whisper in your ear*
*Your mind will interact with my message*
*Stored knowledge is in your head*
*Be silent*
*I will teach you*
*to combine the the histories of all the ages and*
*to spark the modern*
*Notice the symbols on the walls*
*of the old temples*
*They have the answers*
*for the reclaiming knowledge*
*Write your verses O clever one*
*for some will listen with an open ear*
*Dwelling in all times*
*and in all worlds*
*I pick from infinity for you*
*The writings are already written*
*we must only bring them to paper*
*A mastery of soul*

## Shams 8

Our thoughts concentrate on outside things
The poems you write come from inside
and then move outside
an expression for others to feel
Thoughts take place in the past
All revolves around time
Memory lives in the past, present and the future
Soon you will be a memory
of the world you lived in
The past
will be your thoughts that have been written
The present
will be with the reader of your book
The future
are the actions your words will express
going out of the heart
You and I are now creating
Your infinite be-ing
The moment of be-coming a great poet
was never made in this life
It has been inside you
and then at the correct time created
Your energy body is very old
In combination with time and place
there be-comes the poem you write
A spark of imagination
A creation
A poem
And so you give your followers the gift of Hope
Hope a concept of the future

## Shams 9

There are sounds at many levels
They pulsate through your body
Each frequency has a responsibility
as well as a reaction
The energy body is keeping you safe
for its shield reaches far into space

You dear friend
dance to the musical frequency you hear
but there are many other frequencies
sending messages
Physical sound heard by your ears
Astral sound a ringing
Sounds at only mind level
Sounds at only soul level
the sound of your true home
where you move to unite with me
The final dance of the soul
then you become me and I become you
From where you stand it takes many years
But where I stand,
life is fleeting like a beautiful flower
that only blooms one day
It needs the symphony of sound for growing
and the one clash of all notes
for the blooming

## Shams 10

Oh! How man is always searching
for truth
Real truth never causes suffering
Fake ideas, ego,all that goes against
mans true nature
You my bird cling like a wallflower
to your old ideas
therefore your fight will be greater
and prolonged
You are busy with ego
and concepts of ignorance
Ego satisfies all illusion
Your life is an illusion
Love of attachments and
instant gratification
When I look into the faces of your students
I see you
dull and average
We will change all that
To grasp the teachings
sparks of enthusiasm must fly
A keen inquisitive mind grasps
the techniques of the universe
There must be pure intent
And then
one will be rewarded
Pure light will pour into the mind
and heart

## Shams 11

*The keys*
*between time and eternity*
*open different doors, my love*
*The fine point of contact*
*in the human self is …*
*Forgiveness*
*Oh how can you love and kill*
*at the same time?*
*Outside the door*
*man is enslaved by many things*
*he battles to free himself from darkness*
*I will help you to be free*
*by rising above*
*and dancing in a sphere of luminous light*
*It will become a woven cloak*
*a protection for your soul*
*Forgiveness*
*is divine love*
*There are no words for the act of forgiveness*
*It is an energy in itself*
*Forgiveness makes peace*
*through all realms of the earth*
*Forgiveness is a key of gold opening*
*the door of divine understanding*

## Shams 12

Thus the seeds of wisdom fall

Brush away the dust from your eyes
Illuminated sight is set
The only valid truth
is the truth you learn from inside yourself

Since the start of time
I have come to visit
There is never a time
I do not exist
Only my name and body change
as I am manifested in physical form
Freedom of bonds and creeds
are replaced by love and humility
These are the keys
to the souls kingdom of truth
Life and death are senses
of the physical realm and
only as a vehicle for a lifetime
Then oh writer of love
we take residence
in our true home of love
Somewhere in the infinite worlds that
we have not yet traveled

## And so.......

I stand alone, Shams of Tabriz
I am
the law unto myself
I go where I please
I am
the supreme giver
but never the receiver
Time does not bind me
Laws and customs do not rule me
I am
a citizen of the world
Only great love binds me
to all living things
I am
the master and the servant
My love is of complete detachment
for all to feel in their hearts
I am
the soul traveler
giving the instruction
no book will ever reveal

## Good-bye

Oh !How lovely now you have become me
You write poetry to my music of the soul
Knowing words are no longer necessary
Knowing you no longer need me
Oh how you have burned in your dance
Like a moth flying towards the fire
Destroying yourself
Destroying your old beliefs
Separating the spirit from yourself
and
returning in love to a new body
Resurrecting the new energy of love in your heart
Yes, a thousand times yes
to your new poems of love

I love you my bird
40 days and 40 nights
I have filled you with my love

I leave you now for I must wander again
Know your poems will travel like your soul
into infinite time
with my unconditional love

Shams
ليكن

## Cover Artwork

*The cover is artwork from the Blue Mosque*
*Istanbul, Turkey.*
*The mosque was built*
*by Sultan Ahmat the First in 1609.*
*The bird calligraphy dates*
*from the nineteenth century.*
*It is Islamic Calligraphy.*

## Photography

*Blue Mosque Tabriz-, Iran*
*Sultan-Qabus Mosque Muscat, Oman*

# About the Author

By Only human is Peggy Goldreich.
Born in Milwaukee, Wisconsin, USA.
At nineteen, she left America to live in Europe
and became a textile designer
traveling the world.
Her wish came true and she traveled the world,
which had always been her dream.
She met many people and was inspired by
countless things along her path.
The search for insight and empathy for the
beauty and differences in world cultures was
her goal.
Shams
A book that was more or less a channel from
her soul to her head. A piece done for all
to understand that though many things go
unnoticed, truth is buried deep in soul memory
and there is only one truth.

*and so it is*

www.ingramcontent.com/pod-product-compliance
Lightning Source LLC
LaVergne TN
LVHW021343160826
845679LV00008B/1465

*9798891338128*